A Gift For:

....

From:

....

How to Use Your Interactive Storybook & Story Buddy:

1. Press your Story Buddy's ear to start.
2. Read the story aloud in a quiet place. Speak in a clear voice when you see the highlighted phrases.
3. Listen to your buddy respond with several different phrases throughout the book.

Clarity and speed of reading affects Cooper's response. He may not always respond to young children.

Watch for even more Interactive Storybooks and Story Buddies. Available only at Hallmark. For more information, visit us on the Web at www.Hallmark.com/StoryBuddy.

Copyright © 2011 Hallmark Licensing, Inc.

Published by Hallmark Books,
a division of Hallmark Cards, Inc.,
Kansas City, MO 64141
Visit us on the Web at www.Hallmark.com.

Editors: Emily Osborn and Megan Langford
Art Director: Kevin Swanson
Designer: Mark Voss
Production Artist: Dan Horton

ISBN: 978-1-59530-352-3
KOB8000
Printed and bound in China
FEB11

Hallmark
GIFT BOOKS

BOOK 1

Cooper's Big Bear Hug

By **Melissa Woo** • Illustrated by **Crista Couch**

Every day when Cooper woke up,
his mom fixed him a bowl of his
favorite morning honey,
gave him a great big hug, and said,
"Cooper, I love you!"

Of course, Cooper loved his mom
beary much, too, but he wondered
if there was a way to really show her.
He wondered while he brushed his teeth
and combed his fur.

He wondered while he got dressed.
Then Cooper had a great idea!

"I'll ask my friends for help!" he thought excitedly.
"Surely one of them will know the perfect way
to show my mom I love her!"
So Cooper went out to find his friends.
He heard his good pal Finley singing on his front porch.
Finley wanted to be a rock star when he grew up.
But for now, maybe there was a way he could help Cooper.

"Hello, Finley!" said Cooper.
"I was wondering if you could help me
think of a way to show my mom I
love her."

"Hoppy to help!" replied Finley.
"Where I come from, you just can't go
wrong with a necklace of flies!"

Cooper crinkled his nose.

Cooper knew that flies were good
at landing on noses
and they were very good at
getting stuck in his honey,
but making a necklace out of them?
Cooper did NOT want to do that.

Just then, he noticed a small patch of fluffy dandelions. They shimmered in the sun like a garden of pretty jewels.

Suddenly, Cooper had a great idea.

"Wow!" thought Cooper.

"I could make a necklace with the dandelions!"

He imagined they'd look just like a big string of pearls.

But when he went to gather them,

a gust of wind began to blow.

The dandelions twisted and twirled and danced in the air.

They tickled his nose and flew everywhere!

Clearly, this idea was not going to work at all.

He definitely needed a new one.

So Cooper skipped away to find another friend.

It wasn't long before he saw another one of his very best pals, Teeka, scurrying back from the market.

"Hey, Teeka, I need your help!" exclaimed Cooper. "Do YOU know how I can show my mom I love her?"

"Don't be nutty!" laughed Teeka. "All you have to do is bake her a delicious acorn pie!"

Cooper crinkled his nose.

Cooper knew his mom used acorns as earplugs . . .
especially when he played his trombone.
But making them into a pie sounded yucky!
Cooper did NOT want to do that!

He watched as Teeka put away her groceries
and felt a rumble in his tummy.
"I could really use a bowl of berries
right about now," thought Cooper.
Then Cooper had a great idea!

"A berry pie would be just the thing!" he exclaimed.
"Mom loves berry pie!"
So Cooper began searching for berries
next to trees and under rocks.
He even looked in his neighbor's garden.
He found a few that made a nice snack—
but certainly not enough for a whole pie!

"What will I do now?" he wondered.
Even though he couldn't think of
anything, he refused to give up.
Cooper skipped away to find another friend.

Just then, Cooper noticed Sanford
flying high above his head.
"What's up, Sanford?" he shouted.
Sanford was so surprised by Cooper,
he nearly flew into a tree!

After making sure his
feathered friend was okay,
Cooper said, "Sanford, you're
the wisest bird I know.
Can you please tell me how
to show my mom I love her?"

"Goodness' sake!" said Sanford. "There are many, many ways!
Ways as tiny as a fly and others wide as the sky!
But only you'll know the best way for you!"
"Only I'll know?" said Cooper. He already knew that it
wasn't acorns or flies or dandelions or berry pies.

Finally, it came to him.
Cooper had a great idea!

The moment he got home,
Cooper gave his mom the biggest hug
any little bear could give.
After all, her hugs always made
him feel very loved.
Cooper knew he had figured out
the best way to show his mom he loved her.
She hugged him right back and said,
"Cooper, I love you."

DO YOU LOVE USING YOUR IMAGINATION LIKE COOPER? HALLMARK WOULD LOVE TO HEAR FROM YOU!

Please send your comments to:
Hallmark Book Feedback
P.O. Box 419034
Mail Drop 215
Kansas City, MO 64141

Or e-mail us at:
booknotes@hallmark.com